Steck-Vaughn

Think-Alongs™
Comprehending As You Read

Level B

Program Authors

Senior Author
Roger Farr

Co-Authors
Jennifer Conner
Elizabeth Haydel
Bruce Tone
Beth Greene
Tanja Bisesi
Cheryl Gilliland

STECK-VAUGHN
ELEMENTARY · SECONDARY · ADULT · LIBRARY

A Harcourt Classroom Education Company

www.steck-vaughn.com

Acknowledgments

Editorial Director	Diane Schnell
Project Editor	Anne Souby
Associate Director of Design	Cynthia Ellis
Design Manager	Ted Krause
Production and Design	Julia Miracle-Hagaman
Photo Editor	Claudette Landry
Product Manager	Patricia Colacino
Cover Design	Ted Krause
Cover Sculpture	Lonnie Springer
Cover Production	Alan Klemp

Think-Alongs™ is a trademark of Steck-Vaughn Company.

ISBN 0-7398-0084-1

8 9 PO 03

Contents

Thinking About

Picturing Ideas in Your Head

Read the story below. Make pictures in your head as you read.

Beth and her mother went to the swimming pool. Beth put her toe in the water. "It's too cold!" she said.

Her mother said, "The best way to get into cold water is to jump in!"

Beth held her nose and jumped in. She said to her mother, "Come on in! The water feels great!"

What did you picture as you read? Answer the questions below.

I pictured Beth splashing her mother.

- What was Beth wearing?

  _____

  _____

- How did Beth look when she put her toe in the water?

  _____

  _____

What else did you picture as you read?

_____

_____

_____

Read and Think

- Read the stories.
- Stop at each box. Answer the question.
- Picture ideas in your head as you read.

It Happens to Everyone

By Bernice Myers

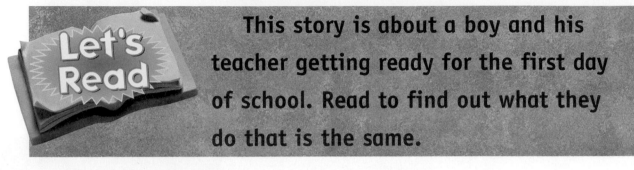

Let's Read

This story is about a boy and his teacher getting ready for the first day of school. Read to find out what they do that is the same.

It's Monday morning. Michael is up early. He's very excited because today is the first day of school. Michael can't decide what clothes to wear.

Mrs. Daniel can't decide what to wear,
either. She's the new teacher, and it's the
first day of school for her, too.

Before breakfast Michael feeds his pets.

 1   What pets do you picture Michael feeding?

Mrs. Daniel gives her cat some sardines.

Michael is in a hurry to get to school. He spills his milk and gets peanut butter all over his sweater.

Mrs. Daniel is in a hurry, too. She spills her coffee.

Michael can't find his other sneaker. He looks at the clock. It's getting late.

Mrs. Daniel can't find her glasses. She looks at her watch. It's already 8 o'clock.

Michael ties his sneaker, grabs his lunch, and runs out the door.

Mrs. Daniel grabs her bag and her briefcase and runs out the door.

The school bus stops in front of Michael's house. He gets there just in time.

2 What do you picture is happening on the bus?

Mrs. Daniel just misses her bus. She has to drive to school in her car.

Michael is a little nervous. He's wondering what school will be like.

Mrs. Daniel is a little nervous, too.

Michael goes into the Boys' Room for a minute. Mrs. Daniel goes into the Ladies' Room.

Michael bumps into a friend. Mrs. Daniel bumps into the principal.

 3 How do you think the principal looks?

Michael looks for his classroom. Mrs. Daniel looks for hers.

Michael hopes the new teacher likes him. Mrs. Daniel hopes her new students like her.

Michael finds his room number. So does
Mrs. Daniel! It's the same one as Michael's.
They go inside together.

"Good morning, I'm Mrs. Daniel, and
this is our first day in school together."

"I'm Michael!"   "I'm Mary!"   "I'm thirsty!"

4 What do you picture on the walls of Mrs.
Daniel's classroom?

Time to Write!

Pretend Michael will be a new student in your class next week. He is a little nervous. You want to help.

- You will write a letter to him to make him feel better.

Prewriting

- First, think about what you want to say in your letter. List three reasons Michael will like being in your class.

1. _____

_____

2. _____

_____

3. _____

_____

Writing

Now, use another sheet of paper to write your letter.

The Doorbell Rang

By Pat Hutchins

This story is about a brother and sister who share their cookies with friends. Read to find out how they have enough cookies.

"I've made some cookies for tea," said Ma.

"Good," said Victoria and Sam. "We're starving."

"Share them between yourselves," said Ma. "I made plenty."

"That's six each," said Sam and Victoria.

"They look as good as Grandma's," said Victoria.

"They smell as good as Grandma's," said Sam.

> **1** What kind of cookies do you picture?

14

"No one makes cookies like Grandma," said Ma as the doorbell rang.

It was Tom and Hannah from next door.

"Come in," said Ma. "You can share the cookies."

"That's three each," said Sam and Victoria.

"They smell as good as your Grandma's," said Tom.

"And look as good," said Hannah.

2 What else do you picture in the dining room?

"No one makes cookies like Grandma,"
said Ma as the doorbell rang.
It was Peter and his little brother.
"Come in," said Ma.
"You can share the cookies."
"That's two each,"
said Victoria and Sam.
"They look as good
as your Grandma's," said Peter.
"And smell as good."

"Nobody makes cookies like Grandma," said Ma as the doorbell rang.

It was Joy and Simon with their four cousins.

 3 What are you thinking about now?

"Come in," said Ma. "You can share the cookies."

"That's one each," said Sam and Victoria.

"They smell as good as your Grandma's," said Joy.

"And look as good," said Simon.

"No one makes cookies like Grandma," said Ma as the doorbell rang and rang.

"Oh dear," said Ma as the children stared at the cookies on their plates. "Perhaps you'd better eat them before we open the door."

"We'll wait," said Sam.

It was Grandma with an enormous tray of cookies.

"How nice to have so many friends to share them with," said Grandma. "It's a good thing I made a lot!"

"And no one makes cookies like Grandma," said Ma as the doorbell rang.

4 Who do you picture at the door now?

Time to Write!

Grandma was good at making cookies. What is something that you do well?

- You will write a journal entry about something you do well.

Prewriting

First, make a list of three things you do well. Then decide which one of the three you enjoy the most and why.

1. I am good at _____ .

2. I am good at _____ .

3. I am good at _____ .

Which of these do you enjoy the most?

_____

I enjoy this the most because _____

_____

Writing

Now, use another sheet of paper to write a journal entry.

The Thinking Place

By Katie U. Vandergriff

This story is about a girl named Megan. She needs to find a quiet place to think. Read to find out where Megan can think.

"I think I need a place to think," said Megan to her sister, Kara.

"What do you need to think about?" asked Kara.

"Things," said Megan. "I like to think about lots of different things."

"Maybe you could go to your room. I go to my room when I want to think," Kara suggested.

"OK, I think I will try to think in my room," said Megan as she rushed off down the hall.

Megan shut her door and sat down on her bed.

1 How do you think Megan's bedroom looks?

As soon as she started to think, she heard a loud noise. THUMP! THUMPA! THUMP! THUMPA! THUMP!

"Oh no!" said Megan. "Christopher is practicing on his drums!" She could not think at all with that noise.

THUMP! THUMPA!

THUMP! THUMPA!

Megan walked out to the garage. She
sat down in her favorite old lawn chair. Just
as she started to think, her dad walked in
the door. "Hi, sweetie, what are you doing?"
he asked.

"I am trying to think," said Megan.

"Well, the garage is a good place. I like
to come here when I need to think, too,"
said her dad with a wink.

---

2 What are you thinking about now?

He walked over to the workbench, put on his safety glasses, and turned on the electric saw. WHEEEEEEENH! Z-Z-ZIP! went the saw as her dad pushed a board into the blade.

"Oh no!" said Megan. She could not think at all with that noise.

Megan walked into the kitchen. She sat down on the stool and sighed.

"What's the matter, darling?" asked her mother.

"I am trying to think," said Megan.

"The kitchen is a good place," said her mother. "I like to think in here." RATTLE, CLANK, RATTLE went the pots and pans. WHIRRRRRRRR went the mixer.

 3 What do you picture Megan's mother wearing?

"Oh no!" said Megan. She could not think at all with that noise. She shook her head sadly and walked out into the backyard.

Megan sat down under the big tree and rested her head in her hands. "Where can I find a place to think?" she wondered. As she sat there, the grass tickled her feet, and she thought how good it felt. Megan lay down on her back in the shade and thought how the tree kept the sun from shining through. She watched the clouds blow by and wondered what made the clouds stay together.

Megan smelled the fresh clover and flowers and thought about what made the flowers grow. She looked up at the big tree and said, "I think THIS will be my place to think!" Megan lay under the big tree and thought and thought and thought.

4 What are you thinking about now?

Time to Write!

What does your "thinking place" look like?

• You will write a paragraph that describes your thinking place.

Prewriting

First, think about what is in your thinking place.

My Thinking Place

Writing

Now, use another sheet of paper to describe your thinking place.

29

Asking Questions

Read the story below. As you read, think about questions you might ask.

It was a cold morning. Kim's father turned on the oven. He got out a bowl. He put in muffin mix, an egg, and water. He stirred it all together. When the batter was smooth, he poured it into a muffin pan. The pan held eight muffins. He put the pan in the oven. Kim's family had hot muffins for breakfast.

What questions did you have as you read? Check the boxes next to the questions you had.

I wondered how long the muffins cooked.

- ☐ What kind of muffins did Kim's father make?

- ☐ How many muffins did Kim eat?

- ☐ What else did Kim's family have for breakfast?

What other questions did you have as you read?

_____

_____

_____

_____

Read and Think

- • Read the stories.
- • Stop at each box. Answer the question.
- • Think about questions to ask as you read.

A Big Brother Knows... What a Little Brother Needs

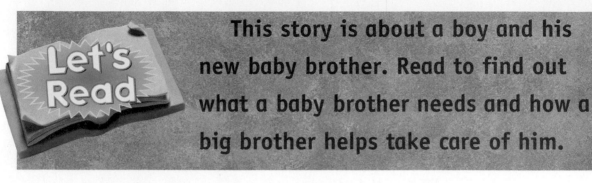

By Vashanti Rahaman

This story is about a boy and his new baby brother. Read to find out what a baby brother needs and how a big brother helps take care of him.

When my baby brother was born, everybody gave him presents—everybody except Daddy.

Daddy gave me a present. He gave me a little music box that played a soft, sleepytime song.

"It's for when you are lonely," he said. "Sometimes big brothers get a little lonely."

"How can I be lonely?" I thought. I was never lonely with just Mama and Daddy. And now there was Baby, too.

At first Baby slept a lot. Sometimes he cried, but Mama always knew why.

Sometimes Mama said, "He is hungry." And when she fed him, he stopped crying.

1 What question do you want to ask the boy?

"How did you know he was hungry?"
I asked Mama.

"I am his mama," she said. "I know."

Sometimes Mama said, "He needs to have his diapers changed." And when she changed him, he stopped crying.

2 What question do you want to ask Mama?

"How did you know he needed changing?" I asked Mama.

"I am his mama," she said. "I know."

Sometimes she said, "His tummy hurts." And she lifted him up, patted his back, rubbed his tummy, and said, "There, there, Mama knows it hurts." Then, after a while, he made a little rumbling, bubbling noise and stopped crying.

3 What question do you want to ask Mama now?

"It's a good thing he has a mama who knows," I said.

Sometimes Mama had to spend so much time with Baby that she couldn't play with me. Then, if Daddy was not home, I got a little lonely. But I had Daddy's music box. When I played it, I felt a little better. I was glad Daddy knew about big brothers getting lonely.

One day Baby kept crying and crying.

Mama fed him.

Mama changed him.

Mama patted his back, rubbed his tummy, and said, "There, there."

But, when she put him down on his play mat, he started crying again.

---

4   What question do you want to ask the baby?

"I think he's lonely," I said.

I got my pillow and lay down next to him.

I played my music box and sang to him.

And Baby stopped crying and laughed a little gurgly laugh.

5 What question do you want to ask about the music box?

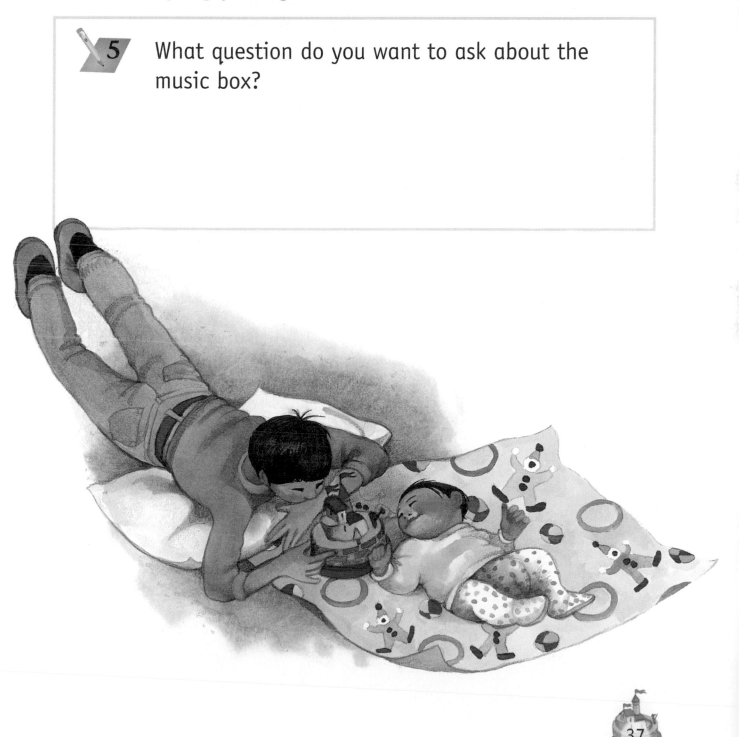

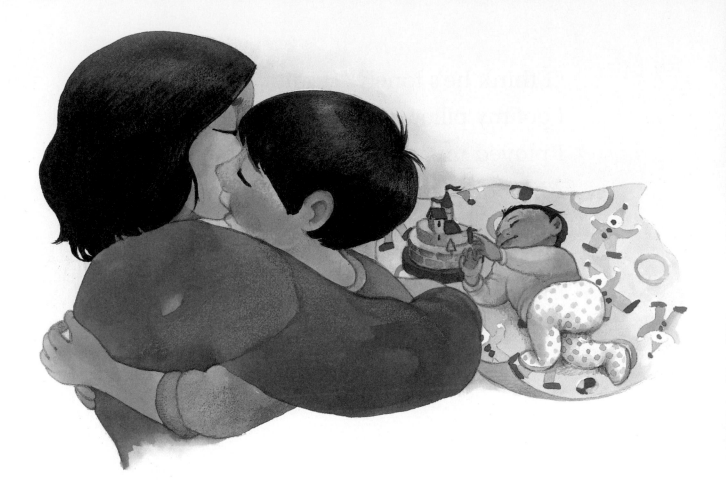

"How did you know that he was lonely?" asked Mama.

"I am his big brother," I said. "I know."

Mama hugged me and gave me a big kiss. "It is a good thing that he has a big brother who knows," she said.

Time to Write!

Think about something that you take care of. It can be your bike, a pet, or a baby brother or sister.

- You will write how to take care of something.

Prewriting

First, answer the questions below.

What do you take care of?

_____

How do you take care of it? Write the steps in order.

_____

_____

_____

_____

_____

Writing

Now, use another sheet of paper. Write about how you care for your special something.

The Statue of Liberty

By Lucille Recht Penner

Let's Read

This story tells how the Statue of Liberty was made. Read to find out what the Statue of Liberty is and how it was made.

A lady stands in the New York Harbor. She is as tall as a skyscraper. She is called the Statue of Liberty.

---

1 What question do you want to ask about the Statue of Liberty?

"Liberty" means freedom. All over the world, people dreamed of coming to America to find freedom.

People came by ship. The trip took many days. Men, women, and children were crowded together. They were tired, hungry, and scared.

Suddenly they saw the lady! They had reached America at last. Now they knew they were free. People cried for joy.

The Statue of Liberty was a present from the people of France to the people of the United States.

A Frenchman made the lady. His name was Frédéric Bartholdi. He copied his mother's face for his statue. How beautiful she was!

 2 What question do you want to ask Frédéric Bartholdi?

First Frédéric made a small statue.
Then a bigger one.
Then an even bigger one.
The last statue was so big it could not
fit in his workshop!

He had to make it in pieces. He made
the right hand holding the torch. Then
he made the head.

Each finger was longer than a man.
Each eye was as big as a child.

Frédéric needed lots of help. His
helpers worked in a big room.

They took the pieces outside and put
them together. She was higher than
all the buildings. Much higher!

Workers took the statue apart. They packed it in 214 crates.

A ship carried it from France to New York. In America the people were building a high pedestal for the lady to stand on.

But they ran out of money! The work stopped. No one knew what to do.

Joseph Pulitzer owned a newspaper. He had an idea.

3 What question do you want to ask about making the statue?

Joseph said, "The statue needs a home! I will print the name of everyone who gives money to help."

Thousands of people sent nickels and dimes. Children sent pennies. Soon there was enough money.

Now workers could finish the huge pedestal. They set the lady on top of it.

 4 What are you thinking about now?

A big French flag was draped over her face.

On October 28, 1886, the people of New York had a parade to welcome her.

The President of the United States made a speech. Frédéric Bartholdi was excited! He raced up a staircase inside the statue. Up and up he went to the very top.

5   What question do you want to ask Frédéric Bartholdi?

Frédéric looked down. A boy was waving a white handkerchief. It was the signal. Frédéric pulled a rope and the flag fell.

There was the lady! Hip, hip, hurrah! Cannons boomed. Boat whistles blew. People cheered.

The excitement never ended. Today, more than one hundred years later, the Statue of Liberty still welcomes people to America— the land of the free.

6 What are you thinking about now?

Time to Write!

The people of France gave the Statue of Liberty to the people of the United States.

- You will write a thank-you note to Frédéric Bartholdi for making the Statue of Liberty.

Prewriting

First, think of all the parts of a thank-you note.

Heading (the date) _____

Greeting (Who is the note to?) Dear _____,

Body (What was the gift? How do you feel about it?)

_____

_____

_____

Closing (such as *Sincerely*) _____,

Signature (your name) _____

Writing

Now, use another sheet of paper to write your thank-you note.

The Case of the Missing Lunch

By Jean Groce

Let's Read

This story is about a young detective named Sam. Read the story to find out how Sam solves the case of the missing lunch.

It was a slow day at the office. There wasn't enough work to do. I needed a case. Something to make me think. Something to make me feel like singing.

Shortly after noon, I heard someone at the door.

It was a boy I knew. He looked sad.

48

"I need your help," he said.

"You've come to the right place!" I sang.

"Got a problem?

Lost your cat?

Sam can find it

just like that!"

1 What question do you want to ask Sam?

"Tell me about it," I said, taking out my pen. "First of all, what's your name?"

"You know my name," the boy said. "I'm your brother."

"All the same, you have to tell me your name," I said. "That's how it's done."

"All right," he said. "My name is Rick."

I wrote the name on my pad. "Now, Rick, tell me your problem," I said.

"My problem is my lunch," Rick said. "It's gone!"

2 What question do you want to ask Rick?

I wrote *lunch* and *gone* on my pad. "That's not odd," I said. "Lunches are always gone after you eat them."

"I didn't eat it!" Rick said. "I made a big, beautiful sandwich. I went to get a glass of milk. When I came back to the table, the sandwich was gone! Can you help me find my lunch?"

"Sure!" I sang.

"In a pickle? In a jam?

The one you need to call is Sam!"

Rick put his hands over his ears. "That is enough singing!" he said. "Your songs are too silly!"

"Sorry," I said. "I always sing. I can't help it. Anyway, let's go."

"Where are we going?" Rick asked.

"To see your plate," I told him. "Show me where you eat lunch."

Rick started to laugh. "You know where I eat lunch," he said. "You live in the same house!"

"All the same, you have to take me there. That's how it's done."

Rick and I went home. There was the plate on the table. I gave it a long look. I didn't see a sandwich.

"I hope you find my sandwich soon," Rick said. "I'm hungry!"

I needed an idea, and I needed it fast.

I looked around. Soon I had seen what I was looking for.

> **4** What question do you want to ask Sam?

I ran next door to borrow three things. Then I ran back home.

"I think I know where your sandwich is," I called to Rick. "Watch!"

I put some dog food in a dish in front of Happy. He gave it one sniff and went back to sleep.

"I knew it! He isn't hungry because he's already eaten," I said. "I'm sorry about your sandwich, Rick, but Happy ate it! See the peanut butter on him?"

I made Rick a new sandwich. Then I wrote *Case Closed* on my pad while I sang,

"Now you're no longer in a jam.
Aren't you glad you called on Sam?"

 5 What are you thinking about now?

Time to Write!

Think of a time you had to find something that was lost or missing.
• You will write about how you found something that was lost or missing.

Prewriting

First, answer the questions below.

What was missing? _____

How did you find what was missing?

_____

_____

Who helped you find it? _____

What other missing things have you found?

_____

_____

How did you find them?

_____

_____

Writing

Now, use another sheet of paper. Write about how you found something that was missing.

Thinking Along on Tests

- Read each story.
- Stop at each box. Answer the question.
- Answer the questions at the end of each story.

What does Grace get for her birthday?

"Happy birthday, Grace!" her brother Adam yelled. "Dad is bringing your present home with him! It's a pet! And it begins with the same letter as your name, *g*."

"Oh!" Grace cried. "What is it?"

1   What are you thinking about now?

"It's not a gorilla!" Adam said.

"Is it a goose?" Grace asked.

"No. It's not a goat, either." Adam winked at Mom.

When Dad got home, he had a big glass bowl. He filled the bowl with water.

Then Dad took out a bag of water with a goldfish in it. He put it into the bowl. The fish swam around and around.

"Oh, goodie!" Grace cried.

"That's a great name," Adam said. "We can call it Goodie."

"No," Grace said. "I will call it Goldie, not Goodie."

"Great!" Adam said, smiling. "Another name that begins with *g*."

 2 What are you thinking about now?

Darken the circle for the correct answer.

1. **Dad is bringing home a**

   _____.

   Ⓐ bicycle

   Ⓑ name

   Ⓒ pet

   Ⓓ picture

2. **Who is having a birthday?**

   Ⓐ Adam

   Ⓑ Grace

   Ⓒ Dad

   Ⓓ Mom

3. **What letter is most important in this story?**

   Ⓐ *h*

   Ⓑ *b*

   Ⓒ *s*

   Ⓓ *g*

4. **Dad's gift was a _____.**

   Ⓐ gorilla

   Ⓑ giraffe

   Ⓒ goat

   Ⓓ goldfish

Write your answer on the lines below.

5. **How does Adam feel at the beginning of the story?**

_____

_____

_____

What is a polliwog?

There is a very old story about a frog. In the story, the frog turns into a prince. But do you know what turns into a frog? It is a tadpole.

A tadpole comes from an egg that a frog lays in the water. A tadpole has a tiny round body with a long tail. It has no legs at first. A tadpole lives under water. It breathes like a fish.

1 What are you thinking about now?

Another name for a tadpole is *polliwog*. The last part of that funny name came from the word *wiggle*. That is how a polliwog, or tadpole, swims. It wiggles its way through the water.

A tadpole and a caterpillar both change into something else. A caterpillar changes into a butterfly. A tadpole changes into a frog.

A tadpole first begins to grow little legs. As its legs grow, its tail gets smaller. It soon has lungs that it will use when it hops out of water as a frog. Finally, a tadpole loses its tail. Then it looks just like a tiny frog.

It is fun to watch a tadpole become a frog. You can't watch a frog become a prince. That is just a story you can read. It never really happens. But you can watch tadpoles turn into frogs!

2 What are you thinking about now?

Darken the circle for the correct answer.

6. Part of the word *polliwog* comes from the word _____.

Ⓐ *swim*

Ⓑ *change*

Ⓒ *tail*

Ⓓ *wiggle*

7. A caterpillar and a tadpole both _____.

Ⓐ become butterflies

Ⓑ turn into princes

Ⓒ change into something else

Ⓓ swim under water

8. A polliwog becomes a _____.

Ⓐ butterfly

Ⓑ frog

Ⓒ caterpillar

Ⓓ prince

9. A frog needs lungs because it _____.

Ⓐ must swim under water

Ⓑ uses them to wiggle

Ⓒ needs them to fly

Ⓓ will hop onto land

Write your answer on the lines below.

10. How does a tadpole change?

_____

_____

_____

_____

What did Sara and Yolanda get at the yard sale?

The people in the neighborhood were planning a yard sale. They wanted to raise money for the new library. Mrs. McCann was in charge. Sara and Yolanda were helping.

Sara and Yolanda wanted to bring some things to sell. But they couldn't think of anything they wanted to give up.

1 What are you thinking about now?

Sara and Yolanda talked about what they could bring to the sale. "I was thinking about giving my baseball glove," Yolanda told Sara. "I haven't used it for a while. But it's the one I used when we won the big game. I just don't think I can give it away."

Sara said she had a game she might bring. "Mom thinks I should give it to the sale. I really like that old game," she told Yolanda. "I played it with my mom and dad and sister and brother. It's too important to give away."

2 What are you thinking about now?

The two girls left each other and went home to look for something for the yard sale. A little while later, Yolanda and Sara were back at Mrs. McCann's house. Yolanda was carrying a baseball glove. Sara had a game under her arm.

"These are the things we want to give to the yard sale," the girls told Mrs. McCann. "We want to help get money for the library."

On the day of the sale, Yolanda's baseball glove sold quickly. She did not see who bought it. Then the girls noticed that Sara's game was gone. Someone had bought it.

After the sale, the girls found out that Sara's dad had bought Yolanda's baseball glove to give to Sara. And Yolanda's mom had bought Sara's game to give to Yolanda.

Yolanda said, "I got your game."

Sara said, "I got your baseball glove."

They both asked at the same time, "Want to trade?"

3 What are you thinking about now?

Darken the circle for the correct answer.

11. What were the people in the neighborhood planning?

Ⓐ a baseball game

Ⓑ a yard sale

Ⓒ a trip to the library

Ⓓ a picnic

12. How did Yolanda feel about her baseball glove?

Ⓐ She wanted to sell it.

Ⓑ She didn't really want to sell it.

Ⓒ She wanted Sara to have it.

Ⓓ She was very tired of it.

13. What did Sara sell at the yard sale?

Ⓐ a game

Ⓑ a box

Ⓒ a baseball glove

Ⓓ a garage

14. Who bought the baseball glove?

Ⓐ Yolanda's mom

Ⓑ Sara's dad

Ⓒ Mrs. McCann

Ⓓ Yolanda

Write your answer on the lines below.

15. Do you think Sara and Yolanda were happy or sad at the end of the story? Why?

_____

_____

_____

Details and Main Ideas

Read the story below. As you read, think about the details and main idea of the story.

Dan has a big red box. He keeps special things inside it. He likes to take his special things out and look at them. He finds the blue ribbon he won for his model car. He looks at the picture of his friend John. Dan sees tiny white sneakers. He wore them when he was a baby. Dan puts everything back in the box. Then he puts the box back in the closet.

special things

Check the boxes next to the special things that were in Dan's box.

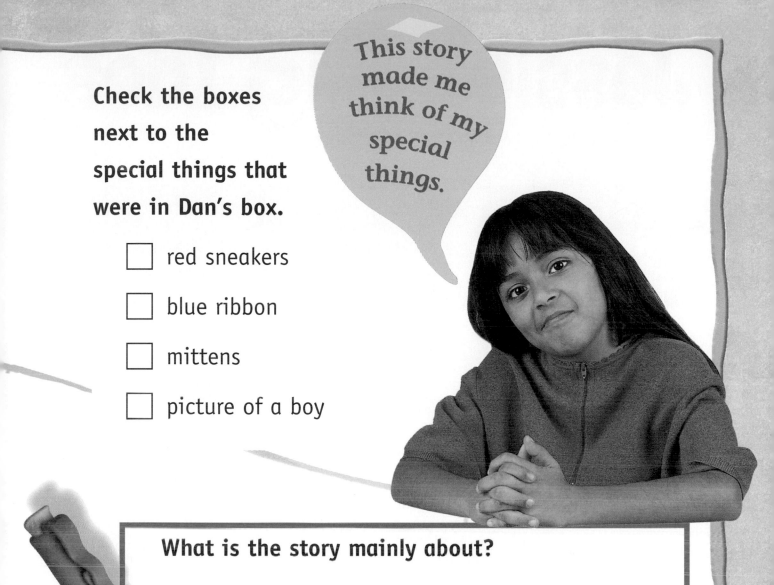

This story made me think of my special things.

- [ ] red sneakers
- [ ] blue ribbon
- [ ] mittens
- [ ] picture of a boy

What is the story mainly about?

_____

_____

_____

Read and Think

- Read the stories.
- Stop at each box. Answer the question.
- Think about details and main ideas.

Jessie's Big Idea

By Carolyn Short

Let's Read

This story is about Jessie. She wants to walk her dog, Bart. Read the story to learn about Jessie's plan to walk Bart.

Jessie loved Bart. She played catch with him. She fed him. She filled his bowl with water. She brushed his shiny coat. She scratched him behind the ears.

1 How did Jessie show that she loved Bart?

Jessie did almost everything for Bart. But there was one thing Jessie couldn't do. She couldn't walk Bart.

"You're too little to walk that big dog," said Dad.

"You can walk him when you're bigger," said Mom.

So every day, Dad walked Bart. Jessie walked with them. When she saw her friend Allison walking her little white poodle, she would smile and say, "Hi, Allison! Hi, Gigi!"

When she saw her friend Conner walking his beagle, she would wave and shout, "Hello, Conner! Hello, Floppy!"

When she saw her friend Mandy walking her cocker spaniel, she would call out "Hello, Mandy! Hello, Ginger!"

If only Bart were as little as her friends' dogs, she would be able to walk him.

2 Why could Jessie's friends walk their dogs?

One day Dad was too sick to walk Bart. "I'll walk him," said Mom. But just as they were leaving, the phone rang. Grandma needed Mom right away.

"I'm sorry, Bart," said Mom. "I guess you won't get a walk today." Bart's tail drooped. Bart's ears drooped. Even Bart's eyes drooped. He stood by the door and whined.

"Poor Bart," said Jessie. "You want to go for a walk, don't you?" She rolled a ball to Bart, but Bart didn't want to play. He lay down on his blanket.

"Poor Bart," said Jessie. "I wish I could walk you." Jessie brushed Bart's back. She brushed Bart's side. She even brushed Bart's tail, but the big dog just stared sadly at the door.

3 Why was Bart so sad?

"Poor Bart," said Jessie. "If I were bigger…" Jessie stopped. She had an idea. She called Allison and Conner and Mandy on the telephone.

The three friends arrived at Jessie's apartment. Each of them carried a leash. Jessie found Bart's leash. She fastened the four leashes to Bart's collar. Bart's eyes sparkled. Bart's ears perked up. Bart's tail wagged.

4 What do you think Jessie is planning to do?

"What's going on?" asked Mom, walking into the apartment.

"Mom, may we walk Bart?" asked Jessie.

Mom looked at the big happy dog and the four happy friends. "What a clever idea," she said. "May I follow along?"

"Yes!" shouted Jessie.

"Woof!" barked Bart.

---

5 How did everyone feel when they went for a walk?

Time to Write!

Think about what happens when Jessie and her friends take Bart for a walk.

• You will write about what you think happens next in the story.

Prewriting

First, draw a picture. Show what Bart will do. Show what Jessie and her friends will do. Will you draw something funny?

Writing

Now, use another sheet of paper. Write about what happens when Jessie and her friends take Bart for a walk.

When Winter Comes

By Pearl Neuman

This story is about what animals do in the winter. Read to learn what different animals do to get ready for the winter.

In some places, when winter comes, it gets very cold. Snow falls on the ground.

People who live where the winters are cold can put on warm coats. They can stay warm in houses, too. They can still get food.

But how do animals in the woods stay warm? How do they get food? What do animals do when winter comes?

1 What do you think this story is going to be about?

Here is a woodchuck with grass in its mouth. It uses the grass to make a nest under the ground.

When it has made the nest, the woodchuck eats lots of the grass and green leaves. By the time winter comes, the woodchuck is fat.

On the very first cold day, the woodchuck goes into its nest. It takes some grass and uses it to plug up the hole to the outside.

Then the woodchuck closes its eyes, curls up in a ball, and goes to sleep.

The woodchuck sleeps all winter long. It sleeps all day and all night. It doesn't need to go out or get up to eat. It lives on its fat all winter long.

 2 How does the woodchuck get ready for winter?

Here is a black bear out for a walk.
Before the first snow, it must find somewhere
to sleep. The black bear looks for a safe
place in a cave or a log. It looks for a good
spot under the trees.

The black bear finds a place to sleep.
Now it is set for the winter. It has a home
where it can spend the cold days. The
black bear sleeps on a grass bed. It
sleeps in the day, and it sleeps at
night, too.

But the black bear does not sleep as long as the woodchuck does. The woodchuck sleeps all winter. The black bear wakes up from time to time. On some days, the black bear leaves its cave and goes looking for plants or animals to eat.

 3 What does the black bear do for most of the winter?

Here is a red fox at work before winter. It digs a deep hole to hide some of its food. It packs away food for the winter, when it is hard to find food.

On a very cold winter night, the red fox will come back to where it hid the food. The fox will dig up the food that it had packed away.

On winter days that are warm, the red fox will go out to look for fresh food. On a walk in the woods, the fox sees a mouse. The red fox dives down in the snow to try and grab the mouse. The mouse can be food for the red fox.

4 What does the red fox do to get ready for winter?

Here are some birds that fly south for the winter. The birds are called Canada geese. When winter comes, they fly south from Canada to Florida or California.

Why do Canada geese fly south? In winter, it is hard for the geese to find food. It is cold and the plants they like to eat stop growing. It is warm in the south. There are plants there for the geese to eat. They fly south to find food.

We know this because people in Canada sometimes put out food for the geese. When they do, the geese stay in Canada for the winter.

In the summer, the geese fly back to the north. In the summer it is hard for the geese to find food and water in the south. It is very dry there. The geese fly north to Canada to find food.

 5   Why do the geese fly south in winter?

What do animals do in the winter? Some sleep like the woodchuck. Some sleep and wake like the bear. Some pack away food like the red fox does. When there's no food, some leave home like the Canada geese.

Each animal does what it needs to do to stay warm and get food when winter comes.

6 What do the animals do in the winter?

Time to Write!

What do you do in the winter? What food do you eat? What clothes do you wear? What games do you play?

• You will write a report telling what you do in the winter.

Prewriting

First, fill out the word web below.

Winter

Writing

Now, use another sheet of paper. Write your report telling what you do in the winter.

85

A Gift to Share

By Barbara Swett Burt

Let's Read

This story is about a girl named Mattie. She wants to give the best gift ever to her Aunt Debra. Read to find out what she gives Aunt Debra.

Soon it would be Aunt Debra's birthday. Everyone in Mattie's family had a present for her, except Mattie. She thought all week about what to give Aunt Debra. She wanted to give her the best gift ever.

Mattie knew Aunt Debra would love a new book. Mattie shook her piggy bank. She had only $1.78. That would not be enough to buy a new book. Mattie thought hard. What could she get Aunt Debra?

1 What do you think Mattie is going to do?

Mattie saw her brother and asked, "What do you think would be the best gift ever?"

He said, "A football, of course."

Mattie said, "Thanks, but I don't think that's the best gift ever." She knew Aunt Debra wouldn't want a football. Mattie thought hard. What could she get her?

Next, Mattie saw her cousin. Mattie asked, "What do you think would be the best gift ever?"

He said, "A car, of course."

Mattie said, "Thanks, but that's not the best gift ever." She knew she couldn't buy Aunt Debra a car. Mattie thought hard. What could she get her?

Mattie ran to the store and found Aunt Debra's favorite magazine. Mattie hoped she would have enough money. But it cost too much. Mattie thought hard. What could she get Aunt Debra?

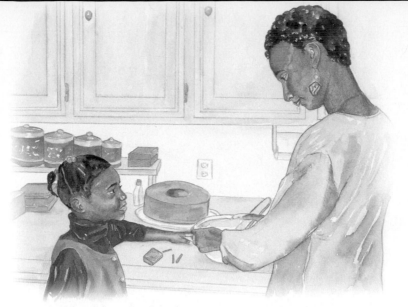

Mattie asked Mom, "What do you think would be the best gift ever?"

Mom said, "Well, sometimes the best gifts are the ones that come from the heart. Could you make something yourself?"

2 What kind of gift could Mattie make?

Mattie thought hard. What could she make? She could make a vase, but she didn't have any clay. She could paint a picture, but she didn't have any paint. She went outside to take a walk and think some more.

She walked toward Aunt Debra's house.
She saw the mail carrier handing two boxes
to her aunt. Aunt Debra said, "Great!
They're here. I've been waiting for my new
books. I just love to read."

Mattie watched Aunt Debra open the
boxes. Her aunt held the books with special
care. Mattie smiled. This gave her a great
idea. She thought, "I can make a book
about me for Aunt Debra to read." She
turned and ran home. She just knew that
would be the best gift ever.

3 What are you thinking about now?

Mattie ran upstairs to her room. She got out her favorite book to see how it was made. Then she got out her art supplies and a box of photos. Mattie picked out her brightest crayons and her best paper. She also picked out some special photos.

Mattie folded the papers. She wrote a title on the first page. She glued photos on the next pages. She printed words in her best writing. She glued her favorite photo to the front for the cover. Then she wrapped the book in pretty paper.

4 What do you think will happen when Aunt Debra sees Mattie's book?

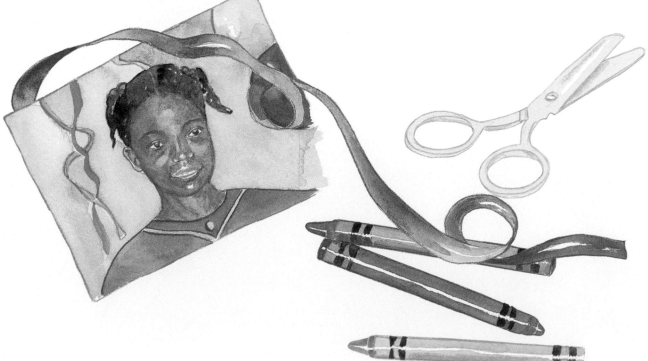

The next day, Mattie gave Aunt Debra her gift. When Aunt Debra opened it, a huge smile filled her face. She said, "This book is so special! It's better than any book I could ever buy." They looked at each photo of Mattie.

Then Mattie had an idea. She found a photo of herself and Aunt Debra sitting together. She glued it on the last page. Aunt Debra looked at the photo and said, "Now the book is about us, too. This is the best gift ever."

5 Why is the book "the best gift ever"?

Time to Write!

Mattie made a special book for Aunt Debra.

• You will make your own special book.

Prewriting

First, think about what you will put in your special book.

Who or what will your book be about? _____

_____

Why is this person or thing special? _____

_____

What pictures can you draw to put in your book?

_____

_____

What can you write to go with your drawings?

_____

_____

Writing

Now, make your own special book.

What Happens First, Next, and Last

Read the story below. As you read, think about what happens first, next, and last.

Aunt Dell makes animals out of wood. First, she cuts the wood to the right size. Next, she shapes the wood to look like an animal. Then, she makes the wood very smooth. Last, she paints the wood. Sometimes she lets me help her paint.

What order did Aunt Dell follow to make the wooden animals? Write 1, 2, or 3 in front of each sentence.

I wondered if she could paint the wood first.

_____ She shapes the wood.

_____ She cuts the wood.

_____ She paints the wood.

What is another step that Aunt Dell does?

_____

_____

_____

Read and Think

- Read the stories.
- Stop at each box. Answer the question.
- Think about what comes first, next, and last.

How Many Stars in the Sky?

By Lenny Hort

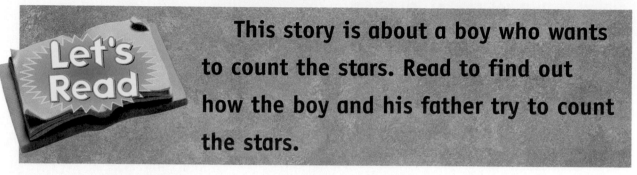

Let's Read

This story is about a boy who wants to count the stars. Read to find out how the boy and his father try to count the stars.

How many stars in the sky?

Mama was away that night and I couldn't sleep. Mama knows all about the sun and stars. But she was away and I didn't want to wake Daddy. So I stared out the window asking myself: how many stars in the sky?

I could count so many just from my room. I leaned out the window and I could count even more. That was just gazing over the backyard. How many stars in the sky?

1 What do you think the boy will do next?

I went outside with a pad and pencil. I started to count. I filled up one whole page of the pad.

But there were lots of stars hidden behind the trees. The house blocked out even more. The streetlamp was so bright I couldn't see stars anywhere near it. How many stars in the sky?

I climbed high up into my treehouse. I started at the Big Dipper and counted in a great circle all around the sky. I filled up page after page of the pad.

2 What makes the boy decide to climb up the tree?

But when I got back to the Dipper it wasn't where I remembered it. I must have been out so long that the stars had moved. Old ones had set. New ones had risen. How many stars in the sky?

I climbed down from the treehouse and there was Daddy. "I couldn't sleep," I said.

"I can't sleep either," he said. "Your mama won't be back till tomorrow."

I told him how I wanted to count all the stars in the sky.

"If your mama was here," Daddy said, "I bet she'd know. Maybe you and I can find someplace where it'll be easier to count them."

My dog hopped in the truck with us and we drove into town. The streets were quiet, but lots of streetlights were burning. We could see the bright city skyline in the distance.

Daddy and I counted twenty-five or twenty-six stars. He said he thought one of them was the planet Jupiter. "This isn't a good place to see stars," I said.

"It's not a bad place to count them, though," he said. "But it's still too hard. Let's go where it'll be really easy."

We drove into the city. The big clock by the tunnel said 2:45, but neither one of us felt like sleeping.

We parked by Mama's office. There was a department store with brightly lit displays in every window. There were streetlamps on every corner.

There were dazzling neon signs.
Headlights flashed from a steady stream of
cars. Powerful searchlights beamed from the
roofs of the skyscrapers.

And I couldn't see any stars at all. "I
count exactly one," said Daddy. "No, wait,"
he said, "it's an airplane."

"Maybe the stars just don't want to be
counted," I said.

We drove back through the tunnel. I was
tired, and I thought we were going home.
But instead, Daddy drove us deep into the
country.

---

3 Why did Daddy drive to the country?

There weren't any cars. There weren't
any streetlights. There weren't any houses.
Even the moon had set. And I knew we
could never count all the stars.

No matter where I looked, new ones
appeared every time I blinked my eyes.
Daddy pointed up above and showed me
the Milky Way. The stars were so thick I
couldn't tell one from another.

We were much too tired to drive anymore,
so we slept underneath the stars that night.

It was daylight when we woke. "Daddy," I said, "all those stars are always out there even when we can't see them, right?"

"Of course they are," he said.

"Can we try to count them again some time?" I asked.

"Any night you feel like it," he said, "you and me and Mama can all go out together."

I could hardly wait to see Mama and tell her about it. In a little while we'd all be back home. But now I was glad just to be standing there with Daddy, basking in the warmth of the one star we could see—and that was the Sun.

4 Did the boy get to do what he wanted during the night?

Time to Write!

The story ends after the boy and his father spend the night counting stars.
- You will write about what you think happens after the boy's mother comes home.

Prewriting

- First, answer the following questions.

Why does the boy wish his mother were home?

_____

_____

_____

What does the boy say he is going to do when his mother gets home?

_____

_____

_____

_____

Writing

Now, use another sheet of paper. Write about what happens the night the boy's mother comes home.

Beaver's Day

By Christine Butterworth

Let's Read

This story is about beavers. Beavers build dams and houses. Read the story to learn how the beavers build their houses.

It is a hot summer day. This beaver is hard at work. It is cutting down trees to make a dam. It bites the trees with sharp, yellow teeth.

Look at these tree stumps. The trees have been cut down by beavers.

The beaver works by a river. It needs the trees to make a dam across the river. It cuts the trees into short logs. It uses the logs to make a dam.

1 What are you thinking about now?

Another beaver comes to help. It takes a log and swims to the dam. It fits the log into the wall of the dam.

The beavers push mud around the logs to keep them in place. They put sticks on the top of the dam. Soon the dam is as high as a tall person.

The beavers use the dam to make a lake. The water in the river is held back by the dam. Soon the water makes a deep lake behind the dam.

> **2** How do the beavers build a dam?

Then the beavers can make their home. Their home is called a lodge.

They cut down more trees to make the lodge. They make a pile of logs in the middle of the lake.

They make two tunnels deep under the water at the bottom of the pile of logs. The other ends of the tunnels come up inside the lodge. The beavers make a room where they can sleep inside the lodge.

3 How do the beavers build their house?

The beavers are hungry after all their hard work. One beaver finds a stick and chews the bark. The other eats some water lily leaves.

This beaver is resting in the sun to dry its fur. Beavers' coats are thick and soft. But their tails have no fur. They are wide and flat. The beavers comb their fur with their claws.

They swim back to the lodge and sit on top of it. They do not see a bear on one side of the lake. The bear is looking for food.

A beaver in the water sees the bear. It smacks the water with its flat tail. Slap! The sound tells all the beavers that there is danger nearby.

4 How does a beaver warn other beavers about danger?

There is a mud slide down the side of the lodge. The beavers slide down it. Splash! They dive deep under the water. They go into the lodge to hide from the bear.

Beavers can swim fast under water. They find the way into the lodge. The tunnel is deep under water. Other animals cannot get in. The beavers will be safe in the lodge.

 5   What do you think will happen next?

The bear looks at the beavers' lodge in the middle of the lake. It can smell the beavers, but it cannot get into the lodge. The bear goes away. The beavers are safe inside the lodge.

Time to Write!

Think about how another animal makes a house. You may have seen a bird build a nest or a spider make a web.

- You will write how an animal makes a home.

Prewriting

First, answer the questions below.

What animal am I going to write about?

_____

What kind of home does the animal make?

_____

_____

How does the animal build a home?

_____

_____

_____

Writing

Now, use another sheet of paper.
Write about how an animal
builds a home.

How Spiders Got Eight Legs

Retold by Katherine Mead

Let's Read

This folktale tells how spiders got eight legs. Read to find out why spiders have so many legs.

Long ago in Africa, spiders had only two legs. There was one spider who was very selfish. He wanted to be better than all the other animals in the jungle. But he did not like to work hard.

Every year, there was a big race in the jungle. All the animals wanted to win. They practiced running every day.

Spider thought, "I am much better than the others. I'll think of a way to win this year's race without working hard."

1 What does Spider want to happen?

Spider watched all the animals run. He thought that Ostrich, Giraffe, or Cheetah could win the race. Spider could not run as fast as any of them. But he did not worry. He had a plan.

Spider thought, "Ostrich has such strong legs. If I had legs like his, I could win the race." Spider went to the river to see Great Hippo, the hippopotamus. He was the wisest animal. He could grant wishes.

Spider called out, "Great Hippo, I wish to have strong legs like Ostrich."

"Why do you wish to have legs like Ostrich?" Great Hippo asked.

"I have to win the race!" said Spider.

Great Hippo said, "I will give you strong legs, but you must promise me something. One day, I will ask you a question. You must answer honestly."

Spider said, "That will be easy." So his wish was granted.

Spider tried to run on his new legs, but it was too hard. He asked Ostrich for help.

Ostrich said, "Watch, my friend. I'll show you how to run with those legs."

Spider watched, but still he could not run.

Spider was mad. He went back to see Great Hippo. He said, "I cannot run with these legs. I wish to have four long legs like Giraffe."

Great Hippo asked, "Why do you wish to have legs like Giraffe?"

Spider said, "I want to take long steps like Giraffe. I have to win the race!"

2 What are you thinking about now?

Great Hippo said, "I will give you four long legs, but you must promise me something. One day, I will ask you a question. You must answer honestly."

Spider said, "That will be easy." So his wish was granted.

Spider tried to run on his long legs, but it was too hard. He asked Giraffe for help.

Giraffe said, "Watch, my friend. I'll show you how to run with those legs."

Spider watched, but still he could not run.

Spider was really mad. He went back to see Great Hippo. He said, "I cannot run on these long legs. I wish for eight legs."

Great Hippo asked, "Why do you wish for eight legs?"

Spider said, "Cheetah is the fastest four-legged animal. I could run twice as fast as Cheetah if I had eight legs."

3 Why does Spider want eight legs?

Great Hippo said, "I will give you eight legs, but you must promise me something. One day, I will ask you a question. You must answer honestly."

Spider said, "That will be easy." So his wish was granted.

4 What do you think will happen next?

Spider tried to run with eight legs, but it was too hard. He asked Cheetah for help.

Cheetah said, "I don't know how to run with eight legs. I could only show you if you had four legs like me."

Spider was madder than ever. He went back to see Great Hippo again. He yelled, "These eight legs don't work! How am I going to win the race?"

Great Hippo did not answer. He just walked into the river to swim.

Spider made his way home. He was still angry. He sat down and thought very hard. How could he win the race with eight legs? Suddenly, he had an idea! He laughed and went to sleep.

On the day of the race, Cheetah could hear someone yelling for help. He said, "That sounds like Spider. I'll go check on him."

Cheetah ran off to Spider's house. Spider was lying down and crying out with pain.

5 What are you thinking about now?

"Spider, what's wrong?" Cheetah asked.

Spider said, "I am very sick. Take me to see Great Hippo. He'll know what to do."

Cheetah said, "Great Hippo is waiting at the finish line. I will take you to him."

Spider climbed on Cheetah's back. Cheetah began to run as fast as he could. The race had already started. Cheetah was behind all the animals. Spider cried louder with pain. Then Cheetah ran faster.

Cheetah ran past the slowest animals. He ran past faster animals. Then Cheetah ran past Ostrich. He ran past Giraffe. Cheetah ran faster and faster until he took the lead.

Spider could see the finish line. He climbed onto the tip of Cheetah's nose. Everyone cheered as Cheetah crossed the finish line. Great Hippo announced, "Cheetah's the winner!"

Spider yelled, "Wait! Cheetah didn't win. I DID! I crossed the finish line first. I won by a nose!"

Great Hippo looked at Spider. He said, "I have a question. Remember that you promised to answer it honestly. Who REALLY won the race?"

Spider was worried. He knew he had to be honest. He said, "I tried to trick all of you. Cheetah is the real winner."

6 Why did Spider have to be honest?

Great Hippo smiled. He said, "Thank you for being honest. Now I will make those eight legs work just right for you."

From then on, spiders everywhere have had eight legs. And they work just right.

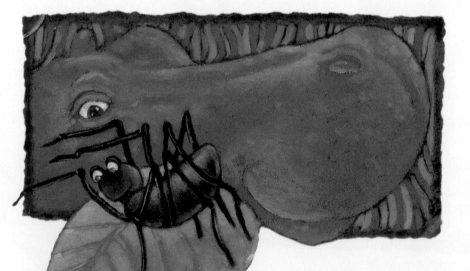

Time to Write!

In this tale, animals talked and acted like people.

- You will write a folktale about animals that talk and act like people.

Prewriting

First, fill in the boxes.

Animals in my story
Story beginning
Story middle
Story ending

Writing

Now, use another sheet of paper. Write your story about animals that talk and act like people.

Thinking Along on Tests

- Read each story.
- Stop at each box. Answer the question.
- Answer the questions at the end of each story.

What happened to Kelly's dog?

"I wish, I wish!" Kelly said.
"I wish that I could have a dog."

"No dogs," Mother said.
"We can't keep a dog here.
A dog would be too hard to
take care of."

Kelly wanted a dog more than anything.
So she drew a picture of a big brown dog.

"Your name is Rover," she told the dog.

 1   What are you thinking about now?

134

Kelly went to sleep with the picture of Rover by her side. She was very happy. But then when she looked at the paper, her dog was gone!

Outside, a man was shaking his rake. "A big brown dog ran through my garden," he said. "Do you own that dog?" the man asked.

"Not me," Kelly said. "We can't keep a dog where I live."

Then Kelly woke up. The picture of Rover was gone. The wind had blown it under her bed. Kelly didn't see it there. "A dog really would be too hard to take care of," she thought.

 2 What are you thinking about now?

Darken the circle for the correct answer.

1. **Kelly gets a dog by**

   _____.

   Ⓐ opening her window

   Ⓑ asking a man for it

   Ⓒ chasing and catching it

   Ⓓ drawing it on paper

2. **Outside, Rover is busy**

   _____.

   Ⓐ making a new friend

   Ⓑ getting in trouble

   Ⓒ chasing cars

   Ⓓ trying to find Kelly

3. **We can tell from this story**

   that Kelly was _____.

   Ⓐ hiding from her dog

   Ⓑ cleaning her room

   Ⓒ having a dream

   Ⓓ talking to her mother

4. **Where is Rover at the end**

   of the story?

   Ⓐ on the picture under the
   bed

   Ⓑ chasing a cat up a tree

   Ⓒ playing in a man's garden

   Ⓓ jumping through the
   window

Write your answer on the lines below.

5. **Why didn't Kelly tell the man that the dog was hers?**

_____

_____

_____

Who is Munchie?

Mother ran up and down the hall.

She was swinging a big straw broom!

She stopped to look in every room,

And Pete could hear her call:

"There's a mouse!

There's a mouse!"

She had spotted poor Munchie

in a minute.

"I won't have a house with a

mouse living in it!

"There's a mouse!

There's a mouse!

There's a mouse in this house!"

> **1** What are you thinking about now?

Munchie ran fast—right past Pete.

He ran down the hall, and then

He ran outside as Dad came in.

He ran away fast on tiny feet.

"Oh, please let Munchie go!" Pete cried.

"He's my friend! I like to watch him play.

He's sure to come back in today.

He doesn't like to play outside."

Mother said, "Then I don't mind at all!

Does he have a horn that he can play?

If he does, then he can stay."

Pete smiled and said, "As I recall,

He plays a piano that's very small."

2 What are you thinking about now?

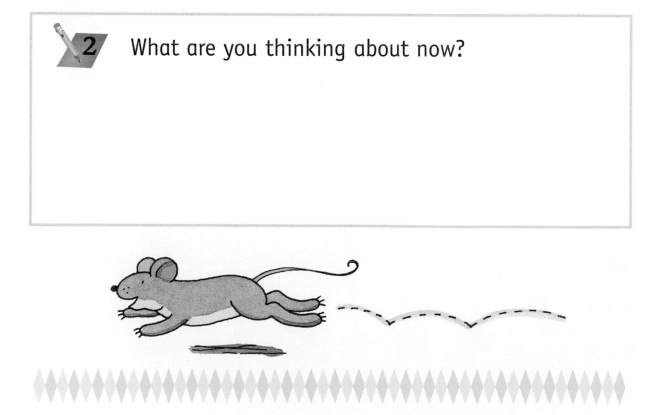

Darken the circle for the correct answer.

6. Munchie is a _____.

   Ⓐ brother

   Ⓑ mouse

   Ⓒ neighbor

   Ⓓ toy

8. In this story, the word *play* means to have fun and to _____.

   Ⓐ make music

   Ⓑ pretend to be angry

   Ⓒ act very silly

   Ⓓ yell loudly

7. Mother is upset because _____.

   Ⓐ Pete is playing outside

   Ⓑ Father is not home

   Ⓒ Munchie is in the house

   Ⓓ Pete is making fun of her

9. When Pete talks about the piano, he is _____.

   Ⓐ joking

   Ⓑ begging

   Ⓒ bragging

   Ⓓ crying

Write your answer on the lines below.

10. How do you think Munchie feels during this story?

_____

_____

_____

_____

Where does Nina go sailing?

The little sailboat sat on Grandpa's desk. It had two pointed sails tied to a center pole. Grandpa said that the pole was called a mast. The sails were white. The boat was a shiny dark blue. The name "Matilda" was painted on each side in tiny white letters.

Nina would sit in the big chair in front of the desk. Grandpa thought Nina was watching him work. But Nina was staring at the sailboat. She would stare until everything around the boat was blurry. She thought the boat was out on a windy sea, and the sails were fat with wind. Nina was on the boat racing across the water. She was captain of the "Matilda."

1 What are you thinking about now?

Finally, one day, Grandpa asked her, "Would you like to have the sailboat?"
"Oh, yes," Nina said.

That day Nina stopped at a pond and put the sailboat into the water. But it would only move a little bit. She tapped it, but it only moved a little bit more. A light wind blew, but the sails did not move. Nina leaned back in the grass and stared. But it was not the same.

The next afternoon Grandpa came into his office and found Nina in the big chair. The little sailboat was on his desk. He did not ask Nina why she had brought it back. He could see Nina staring at the boat. Nina was out to sea again.

2 What are you thinking about now?

Darken the circle for the correct answer.

11. Where is the sailboat at the end of the story?

Ⓐ in a pond

Ⓑ on a chair

Ⓒ on Grandpa's desk

Ⓓ in the grass by the pond

12. What is the name of the sailboat?

Ⓐ Nina

Ⓑ Grandpa

Ⓒ Windy

Ⓓ Matilda

13. What happened at the pond?

Ⓐ The wind blew the boat.

Ⓑ The boat sank.

Ⓒ The boat only moved a little.

Ⓓ The girl fell asleep.

14. In this story, a mast is a _____.

Ⓐ kind of a desk

Ⓑ pole on a sailboat

Ⓒ special chair

Ⓓ strong wind

Write your answer on the lines below.

15. Why did Nina bring back the sailboat?

_____

_____

_____

_____

Acknowledgments

Grateful acknowledgment is made to the following authors and publishers for the use of copyrighted materials. Every effort has been made to obtain permission to use previously published material. Any errors or omissions are unintentional.

Beaver's Day by Christine Butterworth. Copyright © 1990 by Steck-Vaughn Company. Reprinted by arrangement with Macmillan Press Ltd.

"A Big Brother Knows . . . What a Little Brother Needs" by Vashanti Rahaman. Copyright © 1995 by Highlights for Children, Inc., Columbus, Ohio. Reprinted by permission of Highlights for Children, Inc.

The Case of the Missing Lunch by Jean Groce. From SIGNATURES, Grade 2, "The Case of the Missing Lunch," copyright © 1999 by Harcourt, Inc., reprinted by permission of the publisher.

The Doorbell Rang by Pat Hutchins. Copyright © 1986 by Pat Hutchins. By permission of Greenwillow Books, a division of William Morrow and Company, Inc.

A Gift to Share by Barbara Swett Burt. Copyright © 1998 by Steck-Vaughn Company.

How Many Stars in the Sky? by Lenny Hort. Text copyright © 1991 by Lenny Hort. Illustrations copyright © 1991 by James Ransome. By permission of Tambourine Books, a division of William Morrow and Company, Inc.

How Spiders Got Eight Legs retold by Katherine Mead. Copyright © 1998 by Steck-Vaughn Company.

It Happens to Everyone by Bernice Myers. Copyright © 1990 by Bernice Myers. By permission of Lothrop, Lee and Shepard Books, a division of William Morrow and Company, Inc.

"Jessie's Big Idea" by Carolyn Short. Copyright © 1997 by Highlights for Children, Inc., Columbus, Ohio. Reprinted by permission of Highlights for Children, Inc.

The Statue of Liberty by Lucille Recht Penner. Text copyright © 1995 by Lucille Recht Penner. Illustrations copyright © 1995 by Jada Rowland. Reprinted by arrangement with Random House, Inc.

"The Thinking Place" by Katie U. Vandergriff. Copyright © 1996 by Highlights for Children, Inc., Columbus, Ohio. Reprinted by permission of Highlights for Children, Inc.

When Winter Comes by Pearl Neuman. Copyright © 1989 by American Teacher Publications. Reprinted by permission of the publisher.

Illustration Credits

Ken Bowser, pp. 4, 30, 66, 96; Bernice Myers, pp. 6–12; Pat Hutchins, pp. 14–20; Randy Verougstraete, pp. 22–28; Pamela Johnson, pp. 32–38; Jada Rowland, pp. 40–46; John Courtney, pp. 48–54; Ellen Joy Sasaki, pp. 56, 57, 59, 60, 62, 64, 134, 135, 137, 138, 140, 142; Jeff LeVan, pp. 68–74; Richard Roe, pp. 76–84; Béatrice Lebreton, pp. 86–94; James E. Ransome, pp. 98–108; Carol O'Malia, pp. 120–132.

Photography Credits

Cover Sam Dudgeon; pp. 5, 31, 67, 97 Rick Williams; p. 110a ©Don Skillman/Animals Animals; p. 110b ©Gary R. Zahm/ Bruce Coleman, Inc.; p. 111 ©Leonard Lee Rue III/Animals Animals; p. 112 CORBIS/Richard Hamilton Smith; p. 113 ©Perry D. Slocum/Animals Animals; p. 114a ©Johnny Johnson/Animals Animals; p. 114b ©Leonard Lee Rue III/ Animals Animals; p. 115a ©Jonathan T. Wright/Bruce Coleman, Inc.; p. 115b ©Ted Levin/Animals Animals; p. 116 CORBIS/W. Perry Conway; p. 117 ©J.D. Taylor/Bruce Coleman, Inc.; p. 118 CORBIS/W. Perry Conway.